FLORIDA
impressions

P9-BJA-896

photography by James Randklev

FARCOUNTRY
PRESS

RIGHT: Dogwood Spring reflections at Ginnie Springs Recreation Area near the town of High Springs.

TITLE PAGE: Spanish moss on aged cypress trees, Lake Istokpoga near Sebring.

FRONT COVER: Bahia Honda State Park in Florida Keys.

BACK COVER: Alfred B. Maclay State Gardens, Tallahassee

ISBN: 1-56037-229-X
Photographs © James Randklev
© 2002 Farcountry Press

This book may not be reproduced in whole or in part by any means (with the exception of short quotes for the purpose of review) without the permission of the publisher. For more information on our books write: Farcountry Press, P.O. Box 5630, Helena, MT 59604 or call: (800) 654-1105 or visit www.montanamagazine.com
Created, produced, and designed in the United States. Printed in Hong Kong.

RIGHT: At Cypress Gardens.

BELOW: Preening time for a pink flamingo at Homosassa Springs State Park.

FACING PAGE: Fort Jefferson in Dry Tortugas National Park.

BELOW: Tarpon Springs, now a touring center, began as a Greek sponge-fishing village.

ABOVE: Azaleas.

RIGHT: Sunset at Clearwater Pier along the Gulf Coast.

RIGHT: Saw palmettos and palms flourish in Highlands Hammock State Park.

BELOW: A Cooper's hawk finds protection in J. N. "Ding" Darling National Wildlife Refuge on Sanibel Island.

LEFT: Lake Woodruff National Wildlife Refuge.

BELOW: Iris, always a sign of spring.

RIGHT: This Lake Wales grove helps Florida produce three-fourths of the United States' orange crop.

BELOW: At Upper Matecumbe Key, seagrape's brilliant color.

LEFT: Art Deco architecture in Miami Beach's South Beach district.

FACING PAGE: Trolleys deliver tourists to St. Petersburg's Pier of shops and restaurants.

RIGHT: Named by the Spanish for its deep harbor, Bahia Honda Key has been ranked one of the nation's top beaches.

BELOW: An aerial view of the Shark River's channel through Everglades National Park's Ten Thousand Islands area.

Sea oats and fencing help stabilize Gulf Islands National Seashore dunes.

LEFT: St. Marks Lighthouse, built in 1831 along Apalachee Bay on the Gulf Coast, is still in use.

BELOW: The Caloosahatchee River at Fort Myers.

RIGHT: Cedar Key mudflats provide a shorebird's buffet.

BELOW: Bluestriped grunts at Molasses Reef in the Keys.

LEFT: Colorful Art Deco District, South Miami Beach.

BELOW: Elaborate detail in courtyard gardens of Villa Vizcaya Museum built by James Deering (1916) along Biscayne Bay.

LEFT: Tree skeletons on Sanibel Island.

BELOW: Rocket Park at Kennedy Space Center on the Atlantic Coast.

ABOVE: Water lily.

RIGHT: Corkscrew Swamp Sanctuary's old-growth cypress forest thrives in a National Audubon Society Preserve.

FACING PAGE: Cypress trees on Lake Bradford, near Tallahassee.

FAR LEFT: Fort Jefferson's lighthouse, on Garden Key in Dry Tortugas National Park, is nearly two centuries old.

LEFT: This anhinga male hunts for fish by diving deeply from the water's surface.

BELOW: Touring Key West includes views of Bahamian-style buildings.

FACING PAGE: Cape Florida Lighthouse.

LEFT: Fort Lauderdale lifeguard station.

BELOW: The pier at Clearwater reaches into the Gulf of Mexico near Tampa.

FACING PAGE: Ready to surf at Naples.

LEFT: Smathers Beach volleyball at Key West.

BELOW: This ten-inch yellow-bellied slider and his kin are turtles seen at lakes and ponds all over the Southeast.

RIGHT: Springtime at Alexander Springs in Ocala National Forest.

BELOW: The peaceful Blue Spring at Ichetucknee Springs State Park.

Miami hotels fronting the Intracoastal Waterway.

RIGHT: A quiet way to tour manatee waters at Blue Spring.

BELOW: Long Key Beach Park on the Gulf Coast.

LEFT: An Ocala horse ranch.

BELOW: Key deer, the smallest of white-tailed deer, stand about two feet tall and are returning from near-extinction, in the National Key Deer Refuge on Big Pine Key.

FACING PAGE: Pompano Beach.

BELOW: Miami's South Beach is stylish even in its lifeguard stations.

ABOVE: Bok Tower, built in 1928 at Lake Wales, rises among 128 acres of gardens.

FACING PAGE: Historic downtown Daytona Beach.

Blowing Rocks Preserve's limestone outcrops on Jupiter Island.

RIGHT: Fort Clinch at Fernandina Beach was fifteen years old and never occupied when Union troops captured it in 1862. Today it is a Florida State Park.

BELOW: Ponce de León Inlet Lighthouse, Daytona Beach.

LEFT: Seventy miles west of Key West, Bush Key in the Dry Tortugas is a bird sanctuary.

BELOW: Homosassa Spring State Wildlife Park features a viewing room into the protected habitat of manatees, endangered thousand-pound marine mammals that are related to elephants.
© DOUG PERRINE / SEAPICS.COM

RIGHT: A tranquil mood at Jupiter Springs Recreation Area.

BELOW: Magnolias, a symbol of the Deep South.

LEFT: St. George Island State Park, near Apalachicola on the Gulf Coast, provides excellent birdwatching.

BELOW: A Sanibel Island seashell mosaic.

ABOVE: The southernmost house in the United States, Key West.

FACING PAGE: Courtyard of Ringling Museum of Art, Sarasota.

RIGHT: Islamorada Key.

BELOW: A great blue heron in the Everglades.

ABOVE: Bottlenosed dolphins in Discovery Cove.
© DOUG PERRINE / SEAPICS.COM

RIGHT: Spider lilies.

FACING PAGE: The Blackwater River is one of the
world's purest sand-bottomed rivers.

LEFT: Sunset pine forest silhouette at St. George Island State Park.

BELOW: Lake Wauberg at Paynes Prairie State Preserve, near Gainesville.

RIGHT: Moorish-style Henry B. Plant Museum on the University of Tampa campus.

FACING PAGE: St. Petersburg's Don CeSar Beach Resort and Spa, on the National Register of Historic Places, first opened in 1928.

RIGHT: Springs boils at Juniper Springs show where pure water is bubbling from limestone caverns.

BELOW: American alligators live in Florida's freshwater wetlands.

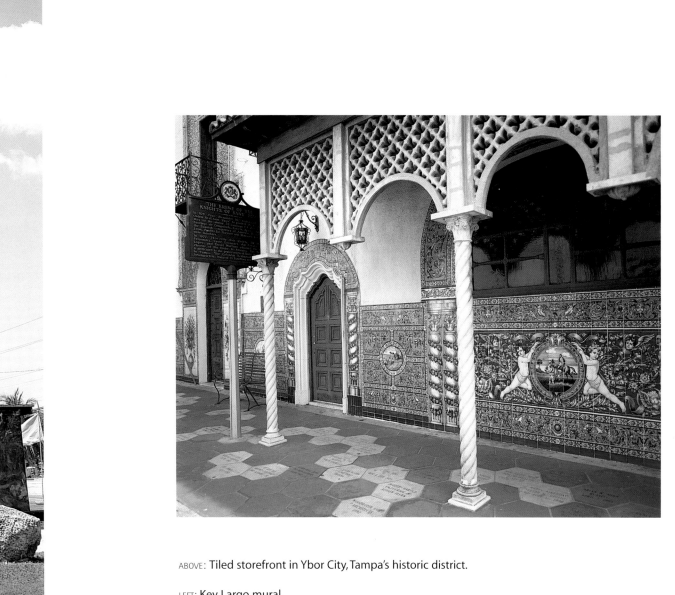

ABOVE: Tiled storefront in Ybor City, Tampa's historic district.

LEFT: Key Largo mural.

RIGHT: St. Marks National Wildlife Refuge covers 90,000 acres in Wakulla County.

BELOW: A Long Key resting spot for pelicans and pals.

FAR LEFT: A blackwater stream flows through The Nature Conservancy's Tiger Creek Preserve.

LEFT: A juvenile alligator amid swamp lettuce, Corkscrew Swamp Sanctuary.

BELOW: Devil's Millhopper State Geologic Site.

ABOVE: In St. Augustine's old-town area.

RIGHT: Castillo de San Marcos National Monument, the United States' oldest masonry fort, was built by the Spanish beginning in 1672.

FACING PAGE: A seagulls' friend at St. George Island State Park.

© MICHAEL HELMS

James Randklev

Master landscape photographer James Randklev has photographed America for thirty years, primarily with a large-format camera that provides the rich images collected in this volume. His brilliant and sensitive work has made him one of the Sierra Club's most published photographers. His color photographs have appeared in books, periodicals, calendars, and advertising—and have been exhibited in shows in the United States and abroad. In 1997, he was the sole American chosen to exhibit in the International Exhibition of Nature Photography in Evian, France. His photography books are: *In Nature's Heart: The Wilderness Days of John Muir; Georgia: Images of Wildness; Wild and Scenic Florida; Georgia Impressions; Georgia Simply Beautiful; Olympic National Park Impressions*; and *Florida Simply Beautiful*.